At the Construction Site

Look, an Excavator!

By Julia Jaske

An excavator can dig up dirt.

An excavator can dig up soil.

4 An excavator can dig up sand.

An excavator can dig up snow.

6 An excavator can dig up gravel.

An excavator can dig up grass.

An excavator can dig
up a trench.

An excavator can dig up a tree.

An excavator can dig up
small rocks.

An excavator can dig
up big rocks.

An excavator can dig up
small holes.

An excavator can dig
up big holes.

Word List

excavator	snow	tree
dirt	gravel	small
soil	grass	holes
sand	trench	big

An excavator can dig up dirt.

An excavator can dig up soil.

An excavator can dig up sand.

An excavator can dig up snow.

An excavator can dig up gravel.

An excavator can dig up grass.

An excavator can dig up a trench.

An excavator can dig up a tree.

An excavator can dig up small rocks.

An excavator can dig up big rocks.

An excavator can dig up small holes.

An excavator can dig up big holes.

CHERRY BLOSSOM PRESS

Published in the United States of America by Cherry Lake Publishing Group
Ann Arbor, Michigan
www.cherrylakepublishing.com

Photo Credits: © aapsky/Shutterstock, cover, 1, 14; © Krashenitsa Dmitrii/Shutterstock, back cover; © xijian/istock, 2; © archimede/Shutterstock, 3; © stevecoleimages/istock, 4; © Marc Dufresne/istock, 5; © ungvar/Shutterstock, 6; © beyhanyazar/istock, 7; © smereka/Shutterstock, 8; © Susan Law Cain/ Shutterstock, 9; © FOTOGRIN/Shutterstock, 10; © David Prahl/Shutterstock, 11; © The world of words/Shutterstock, 12; © naskami/Shutterstock, 13;

Cherry Blossom Press is an imprint of Cherry Lake Publishing Group.

Library of Congress Cataloging-in-Publication Data

Names: Jaske, Julia, author.
Title: Look, an excavator! / by Julia Jaske.
Description: Ann Arbor, Michigan : Cherry Lake Publishing, [2021] | Series: At the construction site
Identifiers: LCCN 2021007853 (print) | LCCN 2021007854 (ebook) | ISBN 9781534188174 (paperback) | ISBN 9781534189577 (pdf) | ISBN 9781534190979 (ebook)
Subjects: LCSH: Earthwork–Juvenile literature. | Excavating machinery–Juvenile literature.
Classification: LCC TA735 .J374 2021 (print) | LCC TA735 (ebook) | DDC 621.8/65–dc23
LC record available at https://lccn.loc.gov/2021007853
LC ebook record available at https://lccn.loc.gov/2021007854

Printed in the United States of America
Corporate Graphics